interviewing your
daughter's date
30 MINUTES MAN-TO-MAN

by dennis rainey
with lawrence kimbrough

FamilyLife Publishing®
Little Rock, Arkansas

Interviewing Your Daughter's Date
FamilyLife Publishing®
5800 Ranch Drive
Little Rock, Arkansas 72223
1-800-FL-TODAY • FamilyLife.com
FLTI, d/b/a FamilyLife®, is a ministry of Campus Crusade for Christ International®

© 2007, 2012 Dennis Rainey
2012—Paperback Edition

ISBN: 978-1-60200-525-9

Design: Brand Navigation, LLC
Cover image of red canvas shoe: © iStockphoto.com/cloki/Igor Skrynnikov
Cover image of brown casual shoe: © iStockphoto.com/Sunny beach

Printed in the United States of America

18 17 16 15 14   1 2 3 4 5

FAMILYLIFE®

I dedicate this book to:

Michael, Jake, and Jason.

Each of you men has received one of the finest gifts I could

ever give . . . one of my daughters. I love you.

Dad R

And to my friend, coach, and encourager, Jerry Wunder.

You were the one who first exhorted me, by your example,

to protect my daughters. I admire your faith and commitment

over the past two decades.

The father of a daughter . . . is nothing but a high-class hostage.

A father turns a stony face to his sons, berates them,

shakes his antlers, paws the ground, snorts, runs them off

into the underbrush, but when his daughter puts her arm

over his shoulder and says, "Daddy, I need to ask you

something," he is a pat of butter in a hot frying pan.

GARRISON KEILLOR
The Book of Guys

Contents

Foreword

Few people have been more helpful to my parenting skills than my friend Dennis Rainey. I'm still benefiting from a particular challenge he gave me years ago when my girls were young:

"Robert, date your daughters. Show them how a real man should act to honor and respect them."

I'm glad I listened. Those dates built priceless memories between my daughters and me.

Here is another high-value move for dads with daughters—the interview. In our community, Dennis is legendary for this.

The guys around here knew the way to Dennis' daughters was *through Dennis*. No, it didn't keep the boys away. But it sure got their attention and, afterward, their respect. Everyone benefited from this simple act of paternal initiative: dad, daughter, and date.

A lot of boys took significant steps toward manhood by passing the interview. And Dennis' daughters have grown to love and admire their daddy *more* because of it.

That, Dad, could be you too.

Robert Lewis
Founder of Men's Fraternity

A joyous moment—walking my daughter Rebecca down the aisle at her wedding. On that day she thanked me for interviewing her dates.

chapter one

She's Still Your Little Girl

There was a day—it doesn't seem that long ago—when this dating stuff was the furthest thing from her mind, back when her only plans for Saturday night were for us to run barefoot together in the mowed grass, playing freeze tag and catching fireflies.

But it turns out I wasn't the only one who would discover how much fun she is to be around.

This little girl I took to magical places in bedtime stories and amazed with tooth fairy notes now has other male voices telling her things a girl likes to hear. This is when a dad, who's never met a monster he couldn't slay, suddenly feels weak and alone.

She's about to go out on a date ... with a boy. Just the two of them.

Should I back off? Avoid the subject? Let my wife handle it? Hope I've done enough?

No. My little girl needs me now more than ever.

Dads, I'm calling you to give your daughter the same strength that once kept you treading water at the base of a diving board. The same sense of protection that kept your hand on the back of her bicycle seat. The same love that pulled her toward you when her friends were mean, when her hopes were dashed. And when life was too big, to her, you were bigger.

> **For most girls your daughter's age, the dating years will lead to heartbreak and confusion, if not utter devastation.**

For most girls your daughter's age, the dating years will lead to heartbreak and confusion, if not utter devastation. Peer pressure and the self-focused nature of needing boyfriends will lead many girls to lose all sense of perspective and make some of the worst decisions of their young lives. That's because most of these girls will be left to fend for themselves by fathers who are too busy, too uneasy, or too afraid to get involved—too quick to assume that everything will be all right. He may know more about the quarterback of his favorite football team than he does about the young man who's driving away with his daughter tonight.

So I'm glad you're reading this book. I'm proud of you for stepping up and out of the herd of men who say nothing and do nothing. It means—at least I hope it means—that your daughter won't have to be one of those girls harmed by relationships that get out of balance and, ultimately, out of hand. It means you are dead-set determined to bring your best effort to this season of your daughter's life—a time that no dad truly feels ready for.

And it means there's at least one more young man out there who's going to have your help building trust, someone who'll be a true gentleman with your daughter, who'll treat her with dignity, the way you want her to be treated.

But first, it's going to take you being a man, because she's still your little girl. And you're still her dad.

This book is fairly short, on purpose. It won't take long for me to say what I need to say, and I don't want you having to stop and start over for days on end. Chances are, you can finish this before you go to bed tonight, or certainly before the week is out.

In the next few pages I'm going to walk you through a brief but vitally important interview process that will make you a little girl's hero and a young man's coach.

At a time when many parents—perhaps even most—are pulling back from their teenage children, becoming less and less involved in what their sons and daughters are doing, you will find yourself—as I have—growing closer to your daughter and deepening your relationship with her, just when she needs you the most.

She may not admit it, but, Dad, your daughter needs you. And so do those guys who think she's cute, who may have every intention of being honorable and aboveboard with her, but who also have truckloads of male hormones surging through their bodies. You can be their protector—both hers and his—keeping them on course toward a life of few regrets.

As a dad, I want to assure you that I did not do everything perfectly. I struggled with balancing work and family. There were times when my patience evaporated, and I was angry with disobedient children. I battled my own inconsistency. Like nearly all dads, I have my own list of regrets. Yet one of my happiest moments came in the summer of 2005 when I had the privilege of being the father of the bride, giving my daughter Rebecca to Jacob William Mutz. On that day, Rebecca had some things she wanted to say to her mom and me. I want you to feel some of what I felt as she spoke these words of tribute. Note especially what she said at the end concerning how she felt about me interviewing her dates.

Dad,

You are, and always will be, my Daddy and my chocolate buddy. I can remember times when you would whisper in my ear to follow you and "sneak some chocolate." I always thought that it was our little secret and our shared moments of bliss. And, of course, it's where I get my love for chocolate.

You have been a source of courage, strength, and godly character. I always knew I wanted to marry someone like you: a man with virtues, morals, character, integrity, a heart after God, and a deep reservoir of love to give me all the days of my life.

I remember putting on my best outfit, fixing my hair, putting on a bit of makeup, and hurrying downstairs to wait for my date. You would sneak out the back door and come around to the front and knock. Mom would answer the door and then call for me, "Rebecca, your date is here." I would walk over, and you would put your arm out for me to take. Then you would escort me to your car and open the door for me, making sure I was safe inside before shutting it. I felt love, honor, and respect in those moments. The rest of the date was a whirlwind, but those moments before and after were the best, as I was taught to wait on you to open all the doors and allow me to walk in front of you. Thank you for showing me what it means to be pursued and treated like a lady.

I could not be more thankful to be standing here today, marrying a man who, is in many ways, like you. What more could I ask for? Thank you for screening all my dates and for doing and saying what you thought was in my best interest, even though it might have been difficult. I cannot tell you how thankful I am for the way you protected me for this moment today. You are a gift from God.

Rebecca Jean "Joy Susie-Q" Rainey Mutz

From one dad to another: It just doesn't get much better than that!

Rebecca and me stepping out for a night of fun.

chapter two

The Neckline, the Waistline, the "Bottom Line"

A dear friend, Pat Orton, who once worked closely with me at FamilyLife, wrote me a letter several years ago, recalling a line her parents had drawn for her as a teenager.

The waistline.

Her mom and dad had told her that whenever she was out with a young man, the only place he was allowed to touch her was on her back, from her shoulder to her waist. Anywhere else on her body was off-limits. And never—never ever—was he to put his hand on her knee.

It was a way for her to know—immediately—if a boy's hands ever strayed out of bounds. And if they did, watch out! This was leading to trouble!

Funny what boundaries can do once they're clearly established. Crossing them is still quite possible, of course, but not without knowing you're doing it, and not without knowing you're breaking trust. And for Pat and her boyfriend-turned-fiancé, this simple, clearly defined rule remained in force throughout their four-year courtship.

Back only. Shoulder to waistline. Nothing further . . . until the day they pulled away from the church on their way to their honeymoon, and he tenderly reached over and placed his hand on her knee.

"I've been waiting four years to do that," he said with a grin.

That's how to start a marriage. Boundaries before marriage bring honor into marriage. And, Dad, you can help your daughter remain honorable and achieve that kind of marriage.

Most likely, you picked this book up because you love your daughter. You're serious about keeping her safe and protected. Yet frankly, you're a bit apprehensive about what can happen to her as she begins dating. For years, I've asked groups of dads how many of them would like their daughters to replicate their own dating experience. Very few hands ever go up.

You may be thinking back to what dating was like for you, especially if you were less than pure in your actions and intentions. You don't want your little girl getting her heart broken or her innocence taken away—like you know it can. Let's be honest: teenage boys can be predators.

As a man, you know the hearts of young men. Their sex drive is at its peak. Life is focused on girls . . . the way they smell, what they wear or don't wear, their legs . . . and other body parts. A young man doesn't understand the hormonal transformation of testosterone, but suddenly it's there, influencing his thoughts. And he wants to be near, very near, a young lady—your daughter!

As one dad put it, "There's an elephant in the room that every man recognizes but few talk about. A young man wants to have sex with my daughter!" Acknowledging the elephant should motivate every father to action.

Perhaps you're concerned that this fatherly responsibility could become a point of contention in your relationship with your daughter. Perhaps you're worried about hovering too closely or risking a backlash. Perhaps you and your wife aren't in agreement right now on the amount of oversight to give.

Perhaps you just don't know what to do exactly.

But to help make your daughter's journey through the dating years a "pure" success, you will need to have a fatherly influence on others, too. The boys who are interested in taking her out, even the ones who come from good families and Christian homes, need more than themselves and their parents to be accountable to.

They can never have too much Dad in their lives.

For eleven years, I taught sixth grade Sunday school to more than seventy young men and women each year. Believe me, it was much more than your usual read-a-verse, tell-a-story, sing-a-song kind of thing. Instead, I talked quite seriously and frankly with these almost-adolescents—not to scare them or grow them up too fast, but to go ahead and get them thinking about things they would be forced to deal with as they headed further into middle school and on into high school.

My goal was to help them set standards for themselves before they came face-to-face with temptation, before the emotional pressure was right up on them, before their peers were pushing them to conform and play along. I wanted to help them craft some convictions that would take some of the guesswork out of their lives later on.

And one of the expectations I established in their young minds was this: If they were ever interested in dating one of my daughters, they could expect to experience (and endure) an initial interview with me. Just the two of us. Man to man.

A decade after I taught my last class of sixth graders, I sat across the table at IHOP downing some syrup-soaked buttermilk pancakes with a young man who had been in that class. Now a junior in college, he had expressed interest in my daughter, and I was doing my daddy duty by conducting a "modified" interview with him. (I'll explain the interview in the next chapter, but, here, let me just say that it changes a bit as your daughter moves into adulthood. By that time, you're talking with men in their twenties, and your interview needs to truly recognize them as men.)

As we began interacting, he broke out in a grin and confessed that a decade earlier, in "that class," he and his buddies had huddled together in the back discussing how the thought of being "interviewed" by me, simply for wanting to date one of my daughters, was one of the worst fears of their young lives!

Yet there we sat with most of his boyish fear set aside, laughing about it. Then I looked him in the eye and had a healthy discussion about being a gentleman and protecting my daughter's innocence. For young men today, I think a little fear is a good thing.

As of today, I've conducted this type of interview with our four daughters' dates somewhere between thirty and forty times. You'll read about some of them in this book.

A few of them have been what you might expect: nervous boys nearly fainting in our living room. These talks have a way of revealing the fact that even wimps can have good taste. Some boys who couldn't last one round in a character contest can at least have the good sense to know a great girl when they see one.

But for the most part, these encounters have allowed me to get to know several young men who would make their parents proud. It's been a little nerve-racking, not just for the boys, but even for me — the one in control, asking the hard questions.

So let's get this out of the way at the beginning: Yes, I was nervous. Every time. But it was worth it. Every time.

Sure, it's been a little rough on my daughters, too. Their friends and potential suitors have always known that the only way to go out with one of those Rainey girls is to talk to her dad first. No doubt there were times when my daughters didn't get asked out when they wanted to, but Barbara and I were willing to help our daughters deal with momentary and occasional disappointment for the sake of long-term good. And this interviewing process is sure to knock out some undesirable dating prospects (not a bad thing).

> **The interview is never meant to be heavy-handed. It's a time when a real man reaches out in a noble conversation about a young lady.**

But to tell the truth, both the advertising and the implementing of these interviews have made me stand a lot taller in my daughters' eyes. And even though it has brought them their share of jokes and teasing, they'd tell you in a minute that they have loved it, even relished it! They've felt good knowing that protecting their innocence and their safety was my priority, something I'd take the time to do. It made them feel valued, protected, cared for, and very loved.

The interview is never meant to be heavy-handed. It's not about an egotistical dad trying to make a teenage boy feel small. It's a time when a real man reaches out to engage a younger man in a noble conversation about a young lady.

Yes, my daughters pushed back on occasion. They weren't always as thrilled about it then as they've become with the value of hindsight. But one of them, who was rebelling and out of our home at the time, brought a boy by for me to interview even though she knew I would disapprove! That's how deep her desire for her daddy's protection and approval went—deeper than her own disobedience. Amazing.

Men, the "bottom line" is this: God made dads to protect their daughters. And one of the ways we can do this is by checking out and qualifying the young men who want to date them.

I've come away from every one of these interview experiences feeling like a real man. But much more important than the way it has made me feel is the benefit to my daughters. They have been spared from most of the predatory passions of even well-meaning boys, as well as the selfish tendencies of their own human natures.

It is one of the most important investments a dad can make in his daughter's life.

Before moving on, I want to acknowledge that it's not just teenage boys who can be predatory. Teenage girls can be, too. In fact, we see this phenomenon more and more in our culture—girls coming on to boys sexually and brazenly. If you've noticed this and you're concerned, good for you for being on guard. I've written a separate book, *Aggressive Girls, Clueless Boys*, to help parents connect with their sons and equip them to know how to navigate dangerous territory.

Yes, your daughter needs you. And so does your son. The trap of immorality is not gender specific.

This baseball bat—named "the Respect Her"—was given to me by a friend who thought an object lesson might add emphasis. It's all in fun, of course, and some of the young men even signed it after our interview.

chapter three

Just You and Me, Kid

I was seated at my desk, barely able to concentrate. I shifted papers, opened drawers, glanced out the window . . . shifted papers, opened drawers, glanced out the window . . . shifted papers . . . I felt like I was expecting an important phone call and was just trying to do something, anything, productive while waiting. But it wasn't working.

And neither was I.

Finally, my executive assistant informed me that the young man I'd been expecting was waiting for me in the lobby.

Deep breath, Dennis. You're the adult here. You can do this.

I was about to interview the first of many young men who wanted a date with one of my daughters.

I stood to my feet and walked across the room, still amazed at how nervous I was as I stepped into the lobby to meet Kevin—the only person in the building more anxious and ill at ease than I was.

"Afternoon, Kevin. Glad you could make it."

"Hello, Mr. Rainey."

"How about we get something from the Coke machine. I hear you're a Dr. Pepper man."

"Yes, sir."

Riding a very thin wave of forced, uncomfortable chitchat, I deposited enough quarters to dislodge a cold can for him and a Diet Coke for me. Then, not wanting to be the "Ultimate Intimidator," I suggested we go outside and chat in the parking lot. That's where he showed me his motorcycle—which wasn't exactly how I wanted Ashley to go out on her first date!

I popped the tab on my soft drink and looked squarely into the same eyes that enjoyed looking at my sixteen-year-old daughter. We began with the basics. I asked him about school, his mom and dad, family, and interests—just a general get-to-know-you type of conversation.

I couldn't believe that my "Little Princess" was already old enough for this. Not my Ashley . . .

I had taken Ashley out myself on numerous occasions when she was younger. I started "dating" her and my other daughters when they were three or four years old.

Sometimes, I'd really try to do it right.

On one specific evening when Ashley was twelve, I pulled into the driveway and met her at the door. Her mother was there to see us off, to inquire about where we were planning to go and when we'd be back. And then we were off.

I, of course, was every bit the perfect gentleman, holding the car door open, ordering for her at the restaurant, and treating her with all the common courtesies a woman should expect from a man.

We just enjoyed ourselves—talking, laughing, and sharing memories. And there were some serious moments, too.

I told her, for example, that I knew she'd one day be asked out by someone much less handsome than her father. (Obviously, we've always enjoyed laughing in our family.) We talked in simple terms about what dating really is and about what she should expect.

I am absolutely convinced that our daughters deeply want this kind of loving attention and protection from us.

I also prepared her for the fact that before she could accept a boy's invitation to go out on a date, I needed the chance to talk to him first. To interview him.

Now, I don't know what you'd expect a twelve-year-old girl to say in response to that, but Barbara and I have enough kids—they qualify as our own little focus group—to assure you that this sounded like a good thing to all my girls, including Ashley that night. It all sounded normal to her.

But even if she hadn't said so, I am absolutely convinced that our daughters—both yours and mine—deeply want this kind of loving attention and protection from us. It makes so many things so much easier on her. It takes a lot of worry off her mind, knowing that Dad is watching her back, keeping her safe by doing his job.

So when the time finally came for Ashley to be asked out by a real live boy, it was only natural for her to say to him, "My dad needs to talk to you first."

That's my girl.

"Kevin," I said, hoping I'd also remember the rest of the words I wanted to say, "God did a wonderful thing when he made women."

The color fell from his face. This was going to be worse than he had thought. I wondered if at any moment he might hop on that motorcycle and bolt!

I continued. "And, Kevin, God made men and women different. You've probably noticed some of those differences."

Kevin was getting paler by the minute, but he had the presence of mind to nod.

"Actually, God made us different so that men and women would be attracted to one another. Now, Kevin," I paused for dramatic effect, "You have probably noticed that God made Ashley quite attractive. She's a really cute girl. In fact, you've probably noticed that she has a cute figure."

This was less of a statement and more of a question. If Kevin said no, he and I would both know he was lying. If he said yes, however, he was admitting to the obvious: that he had the audacity to notice my daughter's figure! Either way, Kevin was "toast."

After a brief pause, I spared him the agony and continued.

"I mean, you're a young man and Ashley is a young lady, and God made men and women to be attracted to one another. It's good."

Kevin seemed to be relieved at my pronouncement.

I went on. "And, Kevin, I just want you to know that I am a man, and I understand this attraction. I was once a teenage boy, and I know what teenage boys think about. I've even read some research on this, and the studies show that teenage boys think about sex every seven seconds."

At this point, Kevin's eyes darted, wondering where I was going next.

"And, Kevin, you and I both know those teenage boys were lying about the other six seconds."

At this point, Kevin's eyes began to dilate! There was no dodging this one. "Yes, sir," he said with a nervous little laugh.

"Kevin, I don't know how to put this any plainer: I want you to keep your lips and hands off my daughter. And I'm going to help you with that. Because whether I see you at the door after your first date with Ashley—or after your fiftieth date—you can expect me to ask you, 'Kevin, are you dealing uprightly with my daughter?' And I want you to know what I mean when I ask you that question. Are we communicating, Kevin?"

"Yes, sir." His eyes were fully dilated at this point.

I continued. "Kevin, more than likely, Ashley is going to be somebody's wife someday. And I don't want you touching her body. Would you want someone touching your wife's body?"

"No, sir."

"That's what I thought. So you and I, we know what we're talking about when I ask you to be accountable for protecting the emotional and moral purity of my daughter, right?"

He nodded enough to let me know my vocabulary was in his dictionary.

"And, Kevin, I want you also to take this challenge: If God ever gives you the privilege of being a husband and a dad, especially if He gives you girls, I want you to take your role so seriously with them that you'll talk to your daughters' dates the way I've talked with you today. Will you promise me that?"

"Yes, sir."

At that point, both Kevin and I were relieved that the conversation was over. I grinned and patted him on the back. I told him I was proud of him for coming to talk to me and allowing me to interact with him around such important issues.

As he was putting his helmet on, he answered one last question by assuring me he'd take Ashley out in a car.

That was it. Took maybe twenty minutes.

And I've done a version of this same thing dozens of times now.

Each interview was a little different. I'll share some of those nuances with you before we're finished. I've learned a lot as I've gone through this. I've learned that there are some very specific things I need to know about each young man, and I try to tailor each of these little talks to the particular situation and the young man I'm dealing with.

In the process, I've met some fine maturing men and seen some interesting things happen along the way.

Here's one that comes to mind. Andy was a young man who had asked to take Ashley to the prom. As I initiated my interview with him, Andy presented me with a Louisville Slugger baseball bat and a black Sharpie pen.

When I asked why he had brought these things, he told me that his dad had sent them so I could write down the major points of what I talked to him about—right there on the barrel of the bat! Andy had a younger sister, you see, who was about to become a teenager, and his dad wanted the outline written down on the bat so he could use it as a cheat sheet for his own interviews with young men—and as a clear visual aid! Andy said his dad intended to hang the bat in the entrance of their home, in fact, as a reminder to all the young men who came to their house.

There was another dad who came with his son to sit in on the interview to observe and be trained. I've also had younger brothers sit in (probably just to see their big brothers squirm).

I even had one young man come to me and say, "Mr. Rainey, I'm not interested in asking any of your daughters out on a date, but I was wondering, would you be willing to take me through the interview?"

I did. He had wanted to go through it so he would know what I said.

It reminded me that young men today yearn for older men to enter their worlds, talk straight with them about how to treat a young lady, and call them to a high standard.

Another dad, Mike, so loved the idea of a father interviewing his daughter's dates, he gave me a baseball bat of my own. He even gave the bat a name and had it laser engraved with two-inch letters etched on the barrel: "The Respect Her." Today, that bat sits on a mantel right above my desk at home. Of course, I'm not advocating violence, abuse, or physical intimidation in any way. The baseball bat is meant only as a humorous symbol of a matter I take seriously. I've heard stories of dads who would clean their guns when young men came over to take their daughters on dates. Personally, I wouldn't feel comfortable doing that. The interview is intimidating enough for any young man. I showed the bat to guys after the interview. It always brought a laugh.

I had no idea until recently while talking to my daughter, Rebecca, that our teenage girls used to show off that bat to their friends. She admitted that she would look forward to having her male friends over to the house and taking them on a brief tour, ending up in my office where she would show them "The Respect Her." Rebecca said she would then tell them that her dad always had to interview her dates. This is the same Rebecca who also pushed back from time to time about "The Interview." With a teenager, expect a paradox from time to time.

Now if all this seems a bit too intense, if the thought of telling your daughter that you'll be interviewing her dates makes you break out in a cold sweat—not to mention the prospect of actually doing the interview—let me tell you how my friend Steve handled it the first time. He calls it "Interview Lite."

When Steve told his two daughters about his plan to interview their dates, they pushed back: "Why do you need to do that? What are you going to say? Will you be kind? Are you going to embarrass us? Are you going to try to intimidate them?"

Steve's responses let them know that he had given this a lot of thought, so they tried a different approach: "What do you consider a date, Dad? Just hanging out with a guy isn't really a date, is it?"

If they were looking for a loophole, they didn't find one. Steve made it clear that a date was anytime a guy and a girl got together—

alone, in a group, and most definitely when just hanging out. But to make it easier on all of them, Steve decided to warm his daughters to the idea by interviewing both their dates at the same time.

For both girls, it was their first date, and they had been invited to a homecoming party. They planned to double date, so Steve invited both of the young men to come to his house for a little chat before the date.

When they arrived, he looked at them, smiled, and asked, "Were you nervous when you asked the girls out?"

Both guys volunteered, "Oh, yeah!"

Steve identified with them by telling them how he had nearly had a nervous breakdown the first time he had asked a girl out in junior high. He then went on to say, "The first thing I want to tell you is thank you for having the courage to ask them. Thanks on behalf of their mother and me. You really did us a big favor by asking both of our daughters out!" (It would have been a long evening if the younger daughter had been asked out but the older daughter had not!)

Steve then asked, "Do you know what stewardship is?" He went on. "You see, we don't own Susie and Emily. We are stewards who have been given an assignment from God to take care of them. And by our letting you take them on a date, we are transferring that stewardship for an evening. You have to keep them safe and healthy and protect their purity." Explaining further, Steve told them, "If a guy comes into the gym with a gun, then I expect you to be a man and take a bullet for them. Are you guys understanding this stewardship? We want you to know that we are holding you accountable for it. Do you understand?"

When Steve was convinced that the young men understood, he shook their hands, and the four teenagers left for the party.

Later, his daughters asked him what he had said to their dates. When Steve told them, they were relieved and said, "That's all? That's great that you'd ask them to protect us like that!" Steve said his daughters' faces were beaming.

By going "Interview Lite" with the first date, Steve earned the early trust of his teenage daughters, who now think the whole thing is pretty cool.

Guys, I can't tell you how strongly I feel about this. The statistics don't lie. Despite a decade of "Just Say No" and countless sermons on "Love, Sex, and Dating," the sexual conduct of Christian youth growing up in Christian youth groups, worshiping to Christian music, and sitting in Christian Bible studies, is virtually no different than the sexual conduct of any other teenager.

These young men who like what they see in our daughters enough to want to spend time alone with them need us to hold them accountable and call them to restrain their sexual passions. They need older men, dads, to challenge them to protect our daughters and do what it takes to guard their moral purity.

Let's do it.

On a date with my four daughters (clockwise from top),
Ashley, Rebecca, Laura, and Deborah.

chapter four

No Daughter of Mine's Goin' Out with a Thing Like That!

The late, legendary Dr. E. V. Hill, longtime pastor of Mt. Zion Missionary Baptist Church in Los Angeles, used to tell the story of a boy who came to his front door one evening, intending to pick up Dr. Hill's daughter for a date.

Something didn't seem quite right about the boy. Maybe it was the way he was dressed, how he carried himself, or how he initially related to Dr. Hill in casual conversation. But Dr. Hill saw warning lights. So while his daughter was still busying herself upstairs getting ready for her night out, he asked the young man some questions about himself, about what he had in mind for that night, and about what he was doing with his life.

By the time his daughter finally appeared, looking and smelling her prettiest, Dr. Hill was sitting on the sofa, reading his paper. Alone.

Her date? He had just left . . . to keep the door from hitting him in the backside.

"Daddy, where's my date?"

"Him? Look, honey, no daughter of mine is goin' out with a thing like that," he answered resolutely.

"Wh-what are you talking about?"

"I said, 'No daughter of mine is goin' out with a thing like that!'"

Disbelieving silence, mouth wide open, "But Daddy, y-you can't just send him away like that! What am I gonna say to him next time I see him? What will they say about me at school?"

Dr. Hill set down his paper, pushed himself to the edge of his seat, and said, "Just a minute here. Let me take a better look at you," squinting his eyes in her direction. "Are you sure you're my daughter?"

"What?"

"Come here a second," he said, getting to his feet, taking her by the hand, and walking toward the kitchen, calling to his wife who was preparing dinner. Stepping inside with his daughter right behind, he said to his bride of nearly three decades, "Help me think now, dear. You're sure there was never anybody else but me? You're absolutely positive that when this girl was conceived, it was you and me? Nobody else?"

"Yeah, baby. Just you and me. She's yours."

"Good. That settles it," he said, turning back to his little girl to make his point clear. "Because no daughter of mine is goin' out with a thing like that!"

You may not be sure a story like this could ever happen in your house, that you'd be quick enough or take that much initiative in one encounter. Would you have the guts to actually forbid an interested party from taking your daughter out, even one time, if you were certain it was the wrong thing to do?

You're not sure you could stand up to him—let alone her!

I don't know how to emphasize this strongly enough: *Protecting your daughter is worth whatever cost or embarrassment or awkwardness it brings.* Take it from those fathers who didn't do enough to protect their girls when they had the chance. Wonder which kind of unpleasantness they'd choose now?

"Okay," you say, "That's good enough for a *why*. But what about *how*? How do I go about starting to protect her?"

> **Your relationship with your daughter will keep your interest and involvement in her dating life from seeming unnatural, out of place, and overbearing.**

Here's how: It is your relationship with your daughter that is the single most important aspect of protecting her. If she feels your love, she'll be more apt to allow you to be her advocate. If she knows you're in her corner, she'll be more open to your role as her defender. Your relationship with her will keep your interest and involvement in her dating life from seeming unnatural, out of place, and overbearing. (Please read that paragraph again. Your relationship with your daughter is that important! Do not try to interview her boyfriend if you don't have a relationship with her!)

That's why I encourage you, even when your daughter is ten, eleven, twelve years of age, to start sharing with her in quiet, casual moments about what to expect when the boys start paying close attention to her. Tell her what the Bible considers to be acceptable behavior when interacting with the opposite sex, especially one-on-one. Before the subject is hot with here and now implications, take the God-given opportunity to talk through this stuff ahead of time, to earn her trust, and to establish the boundaries.

And *especially* let her know how much you love her. Your words aren't meant to smother or threaten, but to encourage her and cause her to feel protected and loved.

But even if it's a little late in her life to implement this kind of pre-game warm-up, if she's already old enough to be dating and you're initiating this process cold, let me give you some encouragement and confidence that you're still doing the right thing. Sitting down with your daughter's dates, even if they've already begun going out together, will give you an opening to actively engage in their relationship. They need to know that you want to be a part of what goes on between them.

Why? Because they need your involvement.

To try to insert yourself in their relationship later, especially at a trouble spot, can come across as heavy-handed. Better to let them know of your intended involvement up front. Otherwise, flare-ups can easily turn into blowups.

I remember a time when one of my daughters was dating a boy named Josh (not his real name). As had become my custom by that time, I had met with Josh one afternoon before they started seeing each other.

I suppose they had been dating for a couple of months when we all went to a football game together. As we were driving home, something told me to glance in my rearview mirror, just to smile and to check on how they were doing back there.

They were sitting pretty close, closer than I wanted them to be. She was in her cheerleader uniform with a skirt that extended a little above the knee. And Josh's hand was on her knee.

I didn't like it. This was not what we had agreed to.

So when we arrived home, I asked Josh if I could speak with him—alone—in the living room. I told him what I had seen, reminded him of what we had talked about, and made it clear that abiding by my expectations was part of the privilege of being able to date my daughter. I didn't beat him up verbally. I spoke respectfully to him, and as far as I know he held the line from that point on.

No, it was not an easy thing for me to do. If, however, I hadn't insisted — before the fact — on having a no-nonsense talk with him, if I hadn't let him know from the beginning that I would be there asking and watching and enforcing my standards, this follow-up moment would have been fifty times more awkward than it was.

It's the difference between a lightning strike that flashes out of nowhere and a storm that's been in the forecast all week. It's being able to communicate with a raised eyebrow instead of a raised voice, with a knowing look instead of a long lecture.

Being there *ahead of time* makes a huge difference.

It not only gives you the right to ask about direct breaches of your purity standards, but also to intercept someone who has simply been untruthful, who hasn't kept his word. I've steered my daughters away from some relationships, not because there was anything sexually improper happening between them, but just because the dynamic was basically unhealthy. Getting to know these young men up front helps you to know more clearly what to watch for and when to step in.

While on a trip to the eastern United States, I met a wonderful couple named Pete and Wanda. In addition to running a company, they operate a mentoring ministry for the youth of Covington, Virginia.

When I met them, I was putting the finishing touches on this book, so the subject was on my mind almost constantly. I guess you could say that my antennae were up for people who could relate to the father-daughter connection, and the better acquainted Pete and I got, the more convinced I became that he might have a story or two. I still remember the life that came to his eyes when I told him about what I was working on.

Turns out that Pete has a daughter and eight goddaughters and that he takes this dad business quite seriously. Not only does he *interview* the boys who ask his daughter out, he *investigates* them, too. When I asked him to explain, Pete told me that he checks into five specific things about each young man. Here is a rundown in Pete's own words:

1. **What is his "credit report" (reputation)?**—*I want to know what kind of reputation the young man has in the community. Every young man has a history, like adults have a credit history, and I want to know what his is, what others—family, friends, school teachers, coaches, etc.—have to say about the kind of person he is. It takes me about five days to do the research on a young man.*

2. **Does he really know God?**—*I want to know if he goes to church, but more importantly, I want to know if he really knows the Almighty. And what impact does the Almighty have on his life?*

3. **What are his educational aspirations?** — *Is he in school now and going to classes? Does he plan to finish high school and take his education further? What kind of grades is he making? Is he taking education seriously? What are his goals?*

4. **Will he protect and provide for my daughter?** — *Does he know how she needs to be protected? Will he treat her like a lady should be treated? If a stranger approaches her, is he willing to put himself in harm's way for her protection? He doesn't have to tell me; I can see it for myself.*

5. **What is his relationship like with his mother?** — *Does he treat her with respect and dignity? I know that how he treats his mother shows how he will treat my daughter. I listen to how he talks to his mom. I want to know, "Does he love his mama?"*

Pete's approach might sound radical, but I think he knows what he's doing. Pete explains, "The generation coming up is basically raising themselves. They need the help of real men."

That's why, in addition to nurturing their own daughter, Pete and Wanda choose to export their love to kids in the community who don't get it at home.

Absentee dads have wounded an entire generation, and I'm glad for a man like Pete who is taking the wheel and redirecting these precious, vulnerable kids. His involvement isn't heavy-handed, it's full-hearted. In my opinion, we need more men like him.

I also want to give encouragement to a group of people who may feel totally outmatched by this responsibility: single moms. (In fact, if you know of a woman who needs to hear this, I hope you and your spouse will share this book with her and support her as she tries to protect her daughters from some of the dangers of adolescence.)

A few years ago I interviewed author Sandra Aldrich on my radio program, *FamilyLife Today*. Sandra's husband had died of cancer at a young age, long before their children had left home. Over the years, Sandra learned to have a very healthy view of what single parents should expect of themselves.

"At first," she said, "I wanted to be the type of mother whose kids give her a dozen roses on Mother's Day and a new crescent wrench on Father's Day. But that was truly naïve because we're not called to be both mother and father to them. We are called to be the best mother or father we can be, and to let God take up the slack."

Yet Sandra knew that the traditional dad role of being the one to stare down the swarming boys, to stand between her daughter and big mistakes as the protector of her virtue, was something she would have to do herself. So she decided to start interviewing each boy when he came to the door, before he and her daughter were allowed to go out.

She would start casually enough, asking him about school and whether he went to church or not. As things turned a little more serious, she could see the little beads of sweat appearing on his forehead. She could sense the miserable knot forming in his stomach. She could spot his frequent glances at the stairs to see when her daughter would appear and end this, not knowing that her girl had been told to wait until "the talk" was over.

That's when the single mom has to stay calm, determined, and brutally honest.

Sandra recalled a time when she said to her squirming captive, "You know, I see you have a nice car out there," pointing toward the window. "What if I asked you if I could borrow your car for the evening?"

A little twinkle escaped from his eyes. The light was coming on. "Uh, I guess I'd have to tell you that maybe I'd have to get to know you a little more first."

"Exactly," Sandra said. "I know you and Holly are just friends, and that's all you're seeing this as, just a friendly date. But, you know, things have a way of getting out of hand sometimes. And I want you to promise me that you're going to treat Holly the way you'd want someone treating your car if you loaned it to them— the way you're hoping another man is treating your future wife tonight."

Single moms, take heart. No one has to remind you that your job is difficult and exhausting, seemingly impossible at times. But whether it's making your home a place where kids can feel comfortable hanging out, helping themselves to the fridge and the pantry, or going out of your way to stay on speaking terms with your children's friends, this is a time when you must make the physical and emotional sacrifices to stay involved in their lives.

> **Please don't send your daughters out there alone, with boys who haven't been warned. You have permission to speak, and you have God's help to do it.**

Single dads, it's the same for you. I know it's tough, especially if you're divorced and, perhaps, don't have primary custody of your children. When you can't always have access to them to develop the kind of relationship you want, the challenge is much tougher. Each encounter with them weighs a little bit more. But the stakes are just as high for your daughter as they are for everyone else. Whatever it takes, stay committed to protecting her.

Please don't send your daughters out there alone, with boys who haven't been warned. You have permission to speak, and you have God's help to do it. Others have done it, and so can you.

It wasn't long after I'd shared the E. V. Hill story with my six children that I decided to take my three younger daughters—Rebecca, Deborah, and Laura—out on a date. I pulled up in front of our house, walked up the sidewalk, and knocked on the door when suddenly my boys, Benjamin and Samuel, appeared in the doorway.

"Excuse me, sir," they said, crossing their arms and looking at me suspiciously. "We have a few questions for you."

"Oh, really?"

"Yeah. We want to know what your plans are. Will you treat these girls like ladies? Will you be a gentleman?"

"Of course," I answered. "I'm their dad, and I intend to take them on a fun-filled, wonderful date."

Not satisfied that I should get off so easily, they kept the questions coming, every now and then breaking into wide smiles and boyish laughter. Finally, after sizing me up for a good five minutes, they looked at each other, nodded their heads and said, "Okay, that settles it. No sister of ours is goin' out with a thing like that!"

And they slammed the door!

It was a really cute moment, but what made it most meaningful to me was this: The message our sons had learned from observing me was that men have a responsibility to protect their daughters.

It's not easy. It's not convenient. It's not always the best way to maintain our popularity and approval ratings at home. But it is our duty and calling, something we can't leave to anyone else.

Protecting our daughters is just what dads do.

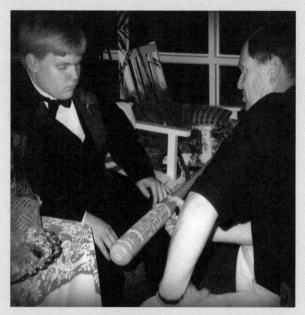

You'll discover—as I did—that interviewing your daughter's date not only protects her, but brings a positive influence to young men.

chapter five

Making Men of Boys

Several years ago, the *Los Angeles Times* (September 18, 1998) carried a story about a group of rambunctious teenage boys.

According to published accounts, a whole group of them had been running wild in a remote section of South Africa, causing major problems and creating huge concerns for those in the area. These docile-looking teens were reported to have been on a rampage in a popular game reserve, killing rhinos as well as charging the cars of safari-goers. They even trampled a German businessman to death as he was trying to rescue his toddler who had fallen out of a car window.

Okay, maybe these were not the same teenage boys you were thinking of at first, the ones who live in your neighborhood, go to your children's school, or run with the church youth group. But they were teenagers nonetheless.

Who were they?

Transplanted teenage orphans. Young male bull elephants.

Zoologists relocated a number of these juvenile pachyderms who had been found abandoned in neighboring game parks. Desperate to give them a change of scenery and another chance at life, their handlers hoped the game reserve in Pilanesberg would produce a calming effect on them, reasoning that older elephants would excite their rebellion.

Instead, these young bulls were coming into sexual maturity ten years earlier than normal and taking out their raging, untamed urges on the white rhinos living alongside them in the bush, while also stalking groups of tourists.

Frantic to restore a sense of order to the Pilanesberg reserve, authorities reversed their thinking and introduced into the population a half dozen *adult* bull elephants, all more than forty years old.

"Hopefully," as one zoologist stated, "the adult bulls will put these young elephants in their place."

And in the six months that followed, there were no reported incidents of trouble between the young elephants, rhinos, and tourists.

What do you make of that?

Everything else in these young animals' lives had stayed basically unchanged: the same vegetation, same weather, same sights, sounds, and seasons.

All these rogue warriors needed was a dad—a little male guidance and leadership.

The reason this whole thing about protecting our daughters resonates with us, the reason almost every dad I speak to automatically sees the *rightness* of it, is that this is a part of our calling as fathers. We know instinctively that defending our daughters, protecting them from danger, and staying in the boat with them through the choppy waters of adolescence, is one of the reasons for our existence.

> **We know instinctively that defending our daughters is one of the reasons for our existence.**

We just know it. Every time I mention this, whether to a few handfuls or a few thousand, everybody gets it. Just like that. Men feel it in their chests.

But leave it to God to double the blessing. When we make the effort to care for our girls, He not only gives us the privilege of protecting them, He doubles the benefit by allowing us to build character into the lives of their dates as well.

I found this out again recently when I was talking to Andy, the young man I mentioned earlier whose dad asked him to bring a baseball bat along to the interview. Andy is in his early thirties now, married with children. He was one of the first young men I interviewed before allowing him to take my daughter Ashley to the prom. The two of them were already friends, and our families knew each other very well, but I still wanted to lay the challenge before him. I owed it to Ashley. Andy was a fine young man, and I owed it to him, too.

Andy came from a great home. He had moral integrity in every way. His father had been and continues to be a wonderful example in his life. Yet the one thing, even now, that lingers in Andy's mind from the brief time we shared together in my backyard that afternoon isn't the baseball bat or the awkwardness he may have felt. He tells me that the most significant thing, second only to the obvious love and care I expressed for my daughter, was my interest in *him*, my concern for *him* as a young man.

Oh sure, he probably wouldn't have said so at the time. He was only eighteen, not exactly an age for deep, introspective thinking. But somehow he understood that I was communicating not just my care for Ashley but my care for him. He had a sense, even at that moment, of being called by an older man to a greater good — to the nobility of being a real man.

He said that our talk made him stand taller.

Now, Andy had no designs toward doing anything improper with Ashley. I remember distinctly when I told him I wanted him to be sure to keep his hands off her body that he quickly said, "Mr. Rainey, I have no intentions there." I knew that. He knew I knew that. But in merely asking the question, by bringing it out in the open with a square look into the eyes and a firm handshake alongside—simply by saying what we were all thinking, instead of avoiding the issue as unapproachable—that moment became a source of courage in his heart. It gave him permission to do what he knew was right. He could feel his chest fill with confidence.

In his book *The Abolition of Man,* C. S. Lewis wrote that the "chest" has traditionally been known as the seat of bravery and will in a man's body. It's the intersecting point of what our heads *know* to do and our bodies *want* to do—the place where raw determination leads to acts of courage and obedience.

Lewis bemoaned the fact that we had increasingly become "men without chests," men without the daring and guts to overcome our self-serving appetites and to be men of integrity, honesty, and purity.

For Andy, our talk made him *feel* like a man—a man *with a chest.*

Part of our job is to help girls become ladies and boys become men. In the words of pastor and author James Merritt, "There is a huge difference between biological reproduction and true fatherhood. One produces a child; the other produces an adult."[1] Dads, we're in the business of making men and women, of helping our children grow up to be adults with clear minds, pure hearts, and

---

1. James Merritt, *In a World of . . . Friends, Foes, and Fools* (Maitland, FL: Xulon Press, 2008), 16.

few regrets. A great deal of their success in life—and I'm not talking about income or job title—will depend on the training they receive from us.

If you make the decision to start interviewing your daughter's dates, you'll be influencing two people at the same time: your daughter and the young man who is interested in her. Naturally, you'll feel a greater responsibility for her at the time, but what a wonderful way to connect with young men and to help them grow.

> **You'll be influencing two people at the same time: your daughter and the young man who is interested in her.**

Mark is one of the young men I connected with. He's a fine man now and I could tell that he would be when I interviewed him several years ago. We've stayed in contact over the years, and when preparing to write this book, I asked Mark what impression the interview process had left on him. His e-mail reply read:

> *From my dating years, one relationship stands out among the rest in health and purity. I don't think it was an accident that this relationship involved a father who was willing to stand as a guardian for his daughter's purity. In order to date his daughter, I had to go through an interview where he laid out the expectations he had for me. This helped me a great deal.*

It imprinted a reminder in my mind that there was a man who cared for this young lady vastly beyond what I did. Not that my feelings weren't strong and real, but the time and love he had already invested in her was unparalleled. So, whenever I found myself in a tempting spot, a vivid picture of this man stood as a protective barrier between me and inappropriate actions.

It not only helped me, but it also made it obvious to the girl how much her dad cared for her. You could sense the great admiration and respect she had for her father since he was willing to offer his strength on her behalf. After having experienced the difference this made in how I treated the girl and the relationship, if I ever have a daughter and some young buck comes knocking on the door, I will not hesitate to sit down eye-to-eye with him and let him know what I expect of him.

Removing the father's role as protector of his daughter and her purity would be like removing the castle wall that guards a princess.

A point of practicality here: Whenever I conduct an interview with a young man, I go in already thinking about what I want to learn about him, his family, and his values. You know as well as I do that there's little room for tolerance and political correctness where our daughters are involved. So I don't feel the slightest bit of hesitation to ask personal questions. Hey, this is my daughter I'm entrusting to his care!

So even though I may not necessarily ask him *all* of these questions, I choose from subjects like these. I'm likely to ask about his:

Family. "Tell me a little about your family. What does your dad do? What does your mom do? How many brothers and sisters do you have? How well do you all get along? What are things like at home?"

Work habits. "Are you working a job anywhere right now? How many hours are you putting in? How do you like it? Do your parents expect you to do much work around the house?"

Life plans. "What do you plan to do in the next few years? College? Work? Military? What are the things that interest you the most? What do you like doing? What's your biggest goal in life?"

Christian testimony. "Do you go to church anywhere? How often do you go? Do you like it? Have you come to a conclusion about who you believe Jesus is? How long have you been a Christian? What difference does Jesus make in your life?"

Driving record. I may even ask about his driving if I happen to be concerned about it. "How many tickets have you received? Ever had a wreck? Ever gotten in trouble with your parents for being irresponsible with your car?"

I also take notice of his overall appearance. I'm not looking for a necktie and matching socks, but I believe a sloppy life often shows itself in the way a young man presents himself to an older man. Check him out. If you met him at the mall, what would you think about him?

I recall one young man that I interviewed who came to meet me wearing a dirty shirt and ragged pants with a huge hole in the knee. It was one of the few times when I didn't go with my gut. I should have told my daughter that she couldn't go out with him, but instead I gave him a second chance. I shouldn't have. Turns out he lied to me.

I look for how the young man handles himself, what kind of manners he shows, the way he answers my questions, the overall attitude he seems to possess, and even the kind of handshake he gives me.

Now, I don't make this a ten-page questionnaire, but based on what I already know about the boy and what my daughter has told me about him, I tailor the interview to him as an individual.

After all, I may be looking at my future son-in-law.

I also know that all the warnings and exhortations in the world won't motivate honorable, respectful behavior in a young man who isn't honorable and respectful to begin with. I need to know that, if I can discern it. (And I have, at times.) This is where prayer is essential. I ask God to guide me and give me discernment as I interact with each young man.

But we should never forget that talking straight with this guy is for his benefit as well. He needs older men in his life. And we can help him, sometimes in ways that even his own dad can't or won't.

I'm sure you've laughed just as hard as I have at the funny stuff that travels around the Internet on this subject. Like the "Application to Date My Daughter" that includes questions like:

> If I were shot, the last place I would want to be wounded is in the _____.
>
> In fifty words or less, what does "late" mean to you?
>
> The one thing I hope this application does not ask me about is _____.

I've also come across a list of "Dad Rules," including such gems as:

1. If you pull into my driveway and honk your horn, you'd better be delivering a package, because you're sure not picking anything up.

2. I'm sure you've been told that in today's world, sex without using some kind of "barrier method" can kill you. Let me elaborate: When it comes to sex, I am the barrier.

3. It is usually understood that to get to know each other, we should talk about sports, politics, and other issues of the day. Please do not do this. The only information I require from you is an indication of when you expect to have my daughter safely back at my house. And the only word I need from you on the subject is "early."

4. As you stand in my front hallway, waiting for my daughter to appear and more than an hour goes by, do not sigh and fidget. If you want to be on time for a movie, you should not be dating. Instead of just standing there, why don't you do something useful like changing the oil in my car?

5. The following places are not appropriate for a date with my daughter: places where there are beds, sofas, or anything softer than a wooden stool; places where there is darkness; places where there is dancing, holding hands, or happiness; places where the ambient temperature is warm enough to induce my daughter to wear shorts, tank tops, midriff T-shirts, or anything other than overalls, a sweater, and a goose-down parka zipped up to her throat. Hockey games are okay. Old folks' homes are better.

Nothing wrong with laughing at these (or for getting some good ideas from a couple of them)! But in God's way of doing things, these valuable moments with young men can truly become mentoring opportunities.

So take this seriously, Dad. It is a high calling, a solemn privilege and challenge. It may not be popular, and it won't be easy. Some will likely oppose you. Your stance may draw some flak—from other parents, in general, because they think you're being a little too over-the-top about this and possibly even from the young man's parents, in particular. They may be quite offended that you seem to be unduly concerned about their son's motives, feeling as though you're questioning the integrity of their family and their boy's upbringing.

> Some of the other families in your church, people who aren't even directly involved, may challenge you for being too strict, for not giving your teenagers "freedom."

Some of the other families in your church, people who aren't even directly involved, may challenge you for being too strict, for not giving your teenagers "freedom." In some situations, you may feel like (or may actually be) the only one who holds this kind of standard. Ours is not a culture, even among those who claim to follow Christ, that wants to do much to restrain the sophisticated freedom of teens.

Because of that, I urge you to see the benefits of doing these interviews, even when met with resistance. What could be worse than letting pressure from others keep you from fulfilling your role as the guardian and protector of the next generation? After all, isn't this one of the very things—not letting outside pressure influence us to compromise our convictions—that we're trying to communicate to our daughters and their dates?

Instead, let this opposition steel your courage to be purposeful. Trust the sense of rightness that wells up from deep within your spirit. And pray that God will guide you to be both encouraging and creative in the way you handle this responsibility.

One time, before a young man by the name of Luke arrived at the house, I gathered all of our most valuable papers and stacked them in a pile on the table that was on our screened-in porch. On this occasion I let my daughter Rebecca join Luke and me for a few minutes. After he and I had worked our way through some preliminary questions, I turned to the pile of valuable documents and began going through them one by one.

I held up Barbara's and my marriage license, my college and seminary degrees and professional certifications, the deed to our house, the titles to our automobiles, various financial statements and retirement investments, a handful of honors and awards, the documentation for just about everything we owned, anything of value.

Then, with my hands still resting on that pile of papers, I looked Luke squarely in the eye and said, "Tell me, Luke, what's the most valuable thing on this porch?"

I'll never forget Luke's face. His eyes were on those papers. Then they began to dart back and forth between that pile, Rebecca, and me. And with a less than confident answer, he said, "Rebecca?"

I affirmed his answer and then went on to share with him that if she was that valuable, then he and I needed to have a little conversation. With that I excused Rebecca.

> **Men, the next generation needs us—the same way we needed godly, older men in our lives when we were coming along.**

Men, the next generation needs us—the same way we needed godly, older men in our lives when we were coming along, men who could have helped us keep the promises we'd made to God and to ourselves. Men whose faces we could have seen in our mind's eye at moments of temptation, men who cared about us enough to ask the tough questions. If you did have men like this in your life, you know what a rare honor and privilege it was. If you didn't, you can surely imagine what a difference it might have made.

Well, today that man is you. You can be "the man" for the young men God brings to your door.

Promise me that you won't chicken out on them.

Deborah and me enjoying a day on the lake. Seems like only a few years ago that my daughters were young and small.

chapter six

It'll Come Back to You

It was Thursday, near noon. Esther had been visiting her parents while her husband was away on business. Since she and the girls—little Carrie and Gracie—would be leaving the next day, Esther's mom had asked if she could have her granddaughters to herself for the day. She had said something about lunch and maybe swinging by the store or the park, things grandmas like to do with such stolen moments.

So while Esther was finishing a crossword puzzle from the morning paper, after picking up the mess caused by their four-day visit, she heard her dad stamping his shoes outside the back door. He had taken these last couple of days off and was taking advantage of the threat of rain in the weekend forecast to get the grass cut early. He came in sweaty and glad to find the pitcher of lemonade his wife had left cooling for him in the fridge.

"Want me to fix you some lunch, Dad?" Esther said, getting up.

"Sure, let's see what we've got in here." In the fridge was mostly juice bags and cookie dough his wife had stocked up on for the grandchildren. So even though his usual favorites took some hunting for, he finally found enough regular stuff to please his appetite.

"Okay," Esther said once the bologna and bread were all out on the counter. "Let me take it from here." She scattered some chips on a paper plate, cut up some celery to add at least a hint of nutrition to the mix, and sat down opposite her dad after pouring him a second splash of lemonade.

How long had it been since he and his little girl had been alone like this—sitting across from each other at the kitchen table, nothing but time on their hands? Why does life nearly force you to wait till they're grown and gone before you see just how special this is?

They chatted awhile about nothing in particular. He said something about how much her mom had looked forward to taking the girls out today. She commented on how nice the lawn looked. He asked her if she'd heard from Jeff, her husband.

"Yeah, he called this morning while you were outside. I think he's had enough. He really sounds ready to get home."

"Well, we sure are glad you all could come up here this week. It's been great to see you again."

He turned back to his sandwich. Esther suddenly felt encouraged to say some words she hadn't really planned to say. She knew this opportunity might never present itself again. Just her and her daddy, with nothing but the hum of the ceiling fan to disrupt the quiet.

"Dad, I know this may embarrass you a little, but just thinking about Jeff brought it to mind."

He set down his lemonade, not sure whether to brace himself or . . . or what?

"Something wrong?" he asked.

"No, no, nothing like that. No, I just, um . . . mean . . . sometimes you don't realize how valuable something is if it's something you've always had, you know, if it's all you've ever known. And, well . . . I'm not sure I've ever really thanked you for making sure I didn't have to learn the hard way."

Dad smiled, still not exactly sure what she was getting at.

"Jeff and I are so happy, Dad. We've been blessed with these girls. And our relationship is just so . . . so much like yours and Mom's. I mean, sure, we get aggravated with each other sometimes. I'm not saying it's like Cinderella and the handsome prince every day. But God has brought us so much joy and . . . unity and . . . we're happy to be together.

"And I owe almost all of that to you, Dad. The way you made sure I knew what I was getting into when I started dating, the way you got involved and held guys accountable. Not too many dads do that for their daughters."

Tears threatened to add a little salt to his celery.

"I mean, you protected me from a couple of relationships I wanted so badly at the time. But looking back, you were so right. They would have been disastrous. I hate to even think about what might have happened if you hadn't stepped in when you did. I know it took a lot of courage, because I was pretty upset with you."

"I remember."

"But you always told me that if I waited, the one God had for me would come along. And he sure did. Jeff was the one for me. You were right.

"But I wouldn't be the same wife for him, Dad, if you hadn't kept me safe the way you did . . . with the others. I hear about all the trouble so many marriages get into, but Jeff's and my relationship with each other is just so sweet and pure and . . .

"I just wanted to tell you that when I say, 'I love you, Dad,' what I mean is, 'I *love* you, Dad.'"

He would have said I love you, too, if he could have talked.

Guys, we make so many decisions in life based on little more than a two- to three-minute time frame. It's so easy and natural to live in no other place than the present. Even with our smart phones and tablet computers, we've got all we can do to keep the roof from caving in before we go to bed at night.

I know. I'm right there with you.

But in thinking about the girls God has given us to guide through life, these precious daughters He has placed under our authority and protection as fathers, we need to free ourselves up to think future tense in our relationship with them—no matter what it may cost us in the present.

We need to think future tense in our relationship with our daughters— no matter what it may cost us in the present.

I'll admit, getting involved in their dating life—both in what they're doing and who they're doing it with—is a serious investment of time and energy. It requires an attentiveness and alertness and willingness to confront—qualities that aren't always left in reserve at the end of a long day, when we'd really prefer to crash in front of the television.

But we're not just dealing with kids here. We're dealing with soon-to-be twenty-five- and thirty-year-old women who will one day look back and see how your love helped them avoid the pain of bad choices—girls who will likely grow up to have their own children to bless with the fruits of their obedience and the joy of promises kept.

So when you start feeling tired of this responsibility, go live in tomorrow for a little while. See a girl who's still got that smile, the one that seems to come from somewhere deep within. Hear that easy laugh that still sparkles with simple innocence. See those eyes that still tell a story of purity, that deep well of strength and honesty that has nothing to hide or to shame her beauty.

One of these days, perhaps over sandwiches and celery, your stance in keeping your daughter's dates accountable may come back to you in floods of gratitude. Or maybe your unwillingness to live in the future when you had the chance will rob you of the experience altogether. I hope not. I pray not.

This is our time, men. The moment we're standing in right now and the one we're hoping for later.

Be there. Both times. She's counting on you.

Well, there you have it. You've heard what I have to say. You've read about my experiences interviewing my daughters' dates. Hopefully, you've been tracking with this, and you sense that it's an important commitment. Your stomach may be tensing up and your hands feeling a little clammy at the thought of it, but you know it's right.

Deep down, you just know it.

So take the next step, and *do it*! You won't regret it. I assure you from years of hands-on practice, the only thing you'll ever regret is not doing it!

If there has ever been a day when dads needed to engage, if there has ever been a time when we could not afford to shrink back but desperately needed to stand up and speak up, if there has ever been a generation of teenagers who needed more of Dad—this is it!

Nothing could be more worthy of fighting for.

So I charge you to report for duty. See this cause for what it is. Realize that the future is very much at stake.

Be the man, Dad.

Be the man.

My wife, Barbara, the love of my life (center top), and my daughters (clockwise), Deborah, Rebecca, Laura, and Ashley. (1999)

The 30-Minute Interview

Use this to remind you of the main points to address in your interview.

1. A woman is God's creation, a beautiful creation, a fine creation.

   You've certainly noticed that my daughter is pretty, attractive, and has a cute figure, haven't you?

2. The attraction of a young man to a young woman is both normal and good.

   I'm glad you like her and want to spend time with her.

3. I understand and remember what the sex drive of a young man is like.

   Believe me, I've been there. I know what you're dealing with.

4. I'm going to hold you accountable for your relationship with my daughter.

Expect me to be asking to see if you're dealing uprightly with her.

5. I'm going to challenge you to purity.

   I want you to guard her innocence, not just her virginity.

6. I want you to respect and uphold the dignity of my daughter by keeping your hands off her.

   Keeping this one precaution in mind will keep you from getting into further trouble.

7. Do you understand all of what I've just said to you?

   Are we clear on what I'm expecting and what you can expect from me?

8. When you're a dad someday, I hope you will challenge your own children to abide by these standards and that you will interview your daughter's dates.

   Can I count on you?

My prayer is that you will never forget this conversation. I know I won't.

A Sample Interview

Your style and approach in conducting these interviews should be your own. Of the dozens of these I've done, although I always cover the eight core points, I vary each one depending on the particular situation and the young man. Here's the way one of these interviews might go:

DAD: Adam, I really appreciate you coming to see me today.

ADAM: Sure.

DAD: We haven't had a chance to meet before now, and I know this may feel a little awkward for you. I'm a little nervous myself, to tell the truth. But I promise you I'm not trying to hurt you or put you through the wringer. It's just really important to me before I allow one of my daughters to date to get to know the person she's going to be with. You understand that, don't you?

ADAM: Oh, yes, sir.

DAD: I mean, if I were to just hand you the keys to my truck, wouldn't you expect me to want to know what you'd be doing with it, where you'd be going, things like that?

ADAM: I guess so.

DAD: Well, I can guarantee you, even though I would sure want to be careful about who I loaned my truck to, I'm a whole lot more concerned about who my daughter is going to be with. And that's why I've decided that having you over here is important. You see where I'm coming from?

ADAM: Yes, sir.

DAD: I've had a number of conversations with young men like you, and each and every time it really ends up being a great time for two men to talk about important matters. It's my belief, Adam, that many parents are giving young people more freedom than they are ready to experience. I also think that my generation hasn't really done the tough work of calling younger men like you to high standards. I mean, this is a challenging culture to grow up in, and I think young men like you need older men in their lives, calling them to be real men.

ADAM: (nodding affirmative)

DAD: Well, first of all, why don't you tell me a little about yourself? You go to school with Sarah, right?

ADAM: Yes, sir.

DAD: Are you both in the same class? You're a senior, too?

ADAM: Yes, sir.

DAD: Have you always lived here?

ADAM: No, we moved here about three years ago for my dad's job and stuff.

DAD: Oh, I see. What does your dad do?

ADAM: He sells, like, um, health benefits to businesses. You know? He's a regional manager, has several people that work for him.

DAD: Hmm. That sounds like a good job. Is that kinda what you have in mind for work yourself?

ADAM: No, I don't think I'd make a very good salesman. I'm hoping to do more like graphic arts or filmmaking, something like that. Maybe music.

DAD: Oh.

ADAM: My brother's more the salesman type.

DAD: Oh, really? You have just the one brother?

ADAM: And a sister, too. I'm the oldest.

DAD: And what about your mom? Does she work outside your home?

ADAM: She works part-time at a doctor's office.

DAD: Oh, I see. Has she always worked? Before you guys moved here?

ADAM: Not till we were all in school.

DAD: Sure, that's a good plan. And you, where have you worked? Are you working anywhere now?

ADAM: Uh, yes, sir. I started working when I was fourteen and have had a part-time job ever since. This summer I'm gonna work for a friend of my dad's who's a contractor. He needed somebody to help clean up on his job sites. Oughta pay pretty good.

DAD: Well, that should be interesting.

ADAM: I guess so. Hot, at least.

DAD: Full time?

ADAM: This summer, yes, sir.

DAD: Right. Have you and your family found a church to go to here?

ADAM: Yes, sir, we go to [name of church].

DAD: Oh, that's a good church. I know a couple of people who go there. You like it?

ADAM: Um-hmm. I sure do.

DAD: What kinds of things do you like best about it?

ADAM: Well, I like the youth group. It's really cool. We have some good Bible studies and stuff. I like the youth pastor and the pastor, too.

DAD: That's good. I'm glad you've been able to get plugged in so quickly around here.

ADAM: Yeah.

DAD: And I assume you're a Christian?

ADAM: Oh, yes, sir.

DAD: I'm always glad to hear that, of course. Our Christian faith is really important to our family, and it is to Sarah, as well.

ADAM: Yeah, I know.

DAD: Tell me a little more about your faith in Christ, what He means to you and how He is working in your life.

ADAM: [Listen for a real answer, not just "church talk" or "Christianese."] Well, I've not always grown as a follower of Christ. I mean, I've tried, but sometimes I just blow it.

DAD: Well, I'll tell you what, Adam, I don't want to keep you much longer, but I do have a few things I always like to tell the young men who ask my daughters out. And the first thing is—and you'll know what I'm talking about, especially since you're a Christian— that God did a wonderful thing when he made women. They are a fine piece of His creation, and they are very beautiful, women are. It's interesting, Adam, that God made two distinct humans, male and female. And He made them different so they would be attracted to one another. This attraction was designed by God, and even God said that it is very good. You know what I mean?

ADAM: Uh, yes, sir. Er, I mean, I guess so.

DAD: In fact, I'd imagine that you wouldn't have asked Sarah out if you didn't think she was kinda pretty. You've probably noticed that she's got a cute little figure, doesn't she?

ADAM: Uh . . .

DAD: It's all right. You can say it.

ADAM: Uh, yes?

DAD: Uh, yes. And being attracted to a young lady like Sarah is a good, normal thing for a boy.

ADAM: (shrugging shoulders, uncertain of what to say)

DAD: You know, Adam, I remember being your age, believe it or not. In fact, I remember it very, very well. I remember seeing girls and thinking about them and wanting to date them. So believe me, I understand what boys think about when they think about girls. In fact, I looked into the matter and found out that teenage boys think about sex every seven seconds. Does that sound about right to you?

ADAM: Uh, well . . .

DAD: You know what I think, Adam? I think whoever did that research was probably about right—except I think those boys were lying about the *other* six seconds!

ADAM: (a little snicker)

DAD: Well, Adam, again, my goal here is not to see how good a job I can do at making you squirm. But I do want to be really clear on the fact that understanding what kind of pressure teenage boys are up against—not just you, but *all* of you—I'm going to hold you accountable for the way you treat my daughter. Okay?

ADAM: Yes, sir.

DAD: And that means, of course, that I'm challenging you to be pure in your dealings with Sarah. You know what I mean when I talk about purity, right?

ADAM: Yes, sir.

DAD: I'm not just talking about not having sex. I'm expecting you to keep your hands off and your lips off Sarah—totally. Okay?

ADAM: (a little slower) Yes, sir.

DAD: See, I want you to respect and uphold her dignity, the same way you'd want somebody to be doing for the woman who'll be your wife someday, if you choose to marry. I mean, more than likely, Sarah is going to be somebody's wife someday, and you're more than likely going to be someone's husband. And even though that may seem a hundred years away to you right now, I want you to hear me very clearly when I tell you how important it is that Sarah be pure for her husband one day, and you for your wife one day. Do you understand?

ADAM: Yes, sir.

DAD: So like I said, that's why I'm promising you—both for your good and for Sarah's—that I will be asking about how you are treating my daughter. Whether I meet you at the door after your first date with her or your *fiftieth* date, you can expect me to ask you more than once, "Adam, are you dealing uprightly with my daughter?" And I want you to know what I mean when I ask you that question. Do you?

ADAM: Yes, sir.

DAD: Okay. Well, listen, I know—again—that this is not the easiest thing for someone to sit and listen to. And you're a good man, Adam, to have made it with me this far. In fact, you can start breathing again now, because I'm almost done.

ADAM: (laughs)

DAD: The last thing I want to tell you is this: If you do get married someday and if you do become a parent and if you do have a daughter, I sincerely hope that you will choose to protect her and remember this little talk we've had. I hope that you'll be as concerned about your daughter's purity and character as I am about my daughter, and that you'll interview any young man who asks to take your daughter out. I mean, now that you've been through my interview, you know how to do it. You think you'll interview young men who want to go out with your daughter?

ADAM: I sure do. And I'll shoot straight with them, just like you did with me!

DAD: That sounds good to me, Adam. This is just very important to me, and even though I know you probably aren't at an age yet where you can fully appreciate where I'm coming from, one day you will be. And I hope you'll never forget this conversation we've had.

ADAM: I won't. I promise you, I won't.

DAD: (looking him squarely in the eyes and extending his hand for a gentlemen's agreement and handshake) May I have your word, as a man, on what we've agreed to here?

ADAM: (extending his hand in confirmation and a firm handshake) Yes, sir.

A Sample Letter to Your Daughter

This can be handwritten to your daughter, or even read to her, as you let her know you plan to interview her dates. Add your own thoughts to help her see that you're doing this because you care about her.

Dear _____,

You're growing up so fast! You're a young lady now and I'm so pleased with the direction your life is going. We haven't agreed on everything—and that will probably always be true about some things—but I want you to know that you make this dad proud.

No doubt some young men are starting to notice you and are hoping to ask you out on dates. This can be a fun time . . . and a scary one. As your dad, I want this time of your life to be enjoyable, safe, and pure. That's why I'm going to be involved. Very involved.

For one thing, before I'll allow a young man to take you on a date, he and I will need to have a one-on-one conversation. I'm not doing this to embarrass you or to intimidate the guy. I'm doing it because I love you. As I said, you're a young lady now and I want to make sure that you're treated like one.

Someday it will be my privilege to put your hand into the hand of another man as you become his wife. Let's work together to make sure that it's the right man.

Your mom and I love you,

Dad

Acknowledgments

In writing any book there are a number of fellow warriors who help an author conquer the "beast." I'd like to say thanks to a few of them.

To Lawrence Kimbrough—you are absolutely masterful. Your help in taking manuscripts, notes, fragments of ideas and even fragments of non-ideas and weaving them into a conceptually sound book are profoundly appreciated. Thank you for your hard work.

To the publishing team at FamilyLife Publishing and the creative design team—Margie Clark, Stephanie Bryant, John Stokes, Michael O'Kane, Rob Tittle, Amy Gordon, Joey Wofford, Rachel Mercer—thank you for your heart, vision, and hard work in making this venture a reality! You are terrific! Thanks!

A special thanks goes to Gregg Stutts for leading the publishing team and stepping into this project courageously. And to Tim Grissom, who helped sharpen the manuscript with his laser-focused editing skills. Both of you are good men for whom I'm grateful to God.

Robert and Andrew Wolgemuth—thanks for your leadership, counsel, and coaching. You are good men.

Janet Logan, Michele English, Todd Nagel, and Merle Engle—thank you for the many ways you helped me juggle the multiple priorities of leading the ministry and launching FamilyLife as a subsidiary at the same time that I was working on this book.

Paula Dumas—you have been a treat to work with—a fresh, talented professional! Thanks for your help and for answering "The Call."

Bill and Tracey Eyster—you two are gifts from God. Thank you for your leadership at FamilyLife. I could never have written this book had you all not decided to join the team! You, indeed, are true difference-makers.

Thanks to Bob Lepine for encouraging me to complete this project.

And to my family—thanks to my daughters, who allowed me to be their daddy. Ashley, Rebecca, Deborah, and Laura—you are *all* gifts from God. It's been a privilege to protect you, guide you, and, yes, interview some of your dates. Yes, I knew about those dates on the side that you thought I didn't know about . . . well, some of them, anyway.

Barbara, thank you for saying yes in 1972 when I asked you to begin this adventure with me! What a journey it's been. *You are the best*!

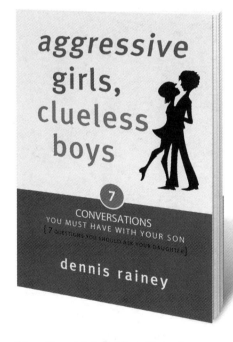

Get away with
your pre-teen for an
adventure of a lifetime!

Passport2Purity® will guide you and your pre-teen through biblical principles regarding peer pressure, dating and sex. Dennis and Barbara Rainey will lead you through this one-on-one retreat with your son or daughter. It's a great time full of discovery, communication and fun.

PASSPORT2PURITY®

1-800-FL-TODAY • FamilyLife.com

GIVE COLLEGE-BOUND KIDS WHAT THEY NEED MOST. 20/20 VISION.

College freshmen head to campus loaded with stuff, but they may be missing the foresight needed for success in college *and* life. This six-video series, complete with student handbook and leader's guide, will prepare high school students for what's ahead. By stressing good habits, smart decision-making and spiritual growth, College Ready provides a plan for success that works. To find out more, visit **CollegeReady.com**.

college ready

1-800-FL-TODAY • FamilyLife.com

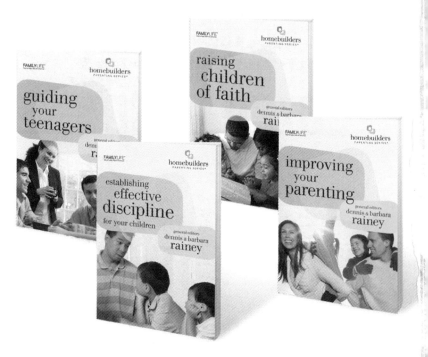

homebuilders
PARENTING SERIES ®

Your family is under construction every day. So gather some friends and dive into the life-changing discussions of the HomeBuilders Parenting Series—full of practical applications for your family. Each 60-minute study is designed for four to seven couples, focusing on one of four real-life topics and biblical truth. Whether you're parenting toddlers, teens, or somewhere in between you can find help and hope for your family.

1-800-FL-TODAY • FamilyLife.com